Lessons

Red Elk

Artwork provided by:
Gary Holland
Shining Mountain Gallery
www.shiningmountainart.com

Edited & Published by:
Heather Dalberg
TKWeb

DEDICATION

To You!

CONTENTS

ACKNOWLEDGMENTS

Thank you to Adam Barbera for supporting this
book and testing the lessons.

HEALTH SERIES

Friend,

    This is to introduce myself to you as well as this lesson. My name is Red Elk. This name was given to me in ceremony; it is not my surname, or family name. I am a half-breed and make no claim to be a full-blood. I am a medicine man - Wakhan of the Inner Heyoka'. Know that the lesson you have here can be found in the Good Book, the Bible. Though most medicine people know how to do these things, this/these are not limited to the Native American world at all. These can be found in a book that is over two thousand years old – lessons included – IF YOU KNOW HOW TO FIND THE LESSONS. In short, what you are paying me for is to do your homework.

    To be successful in most of these lessons, you MUST "get into the child-like mind". This means not an *iota* of doubt. IF any doubt of any kind enters in, you will not succeed. Though you must try to do these, the trick is to enjoy these and have fun. Then you have entered the child-like mind. I wish you well. IT CAN BE DONE. Ho,

Red Elk

The only reason I'm giving these things out, it's not to make money, it's because, one, I'm ordered, number two, these things are going to be needed in the very near future, especially things like Invisibility. For those who are trying to escape the chases, you might be one of the survivors and you've got to disappear. There's no place to go. There's no place to hide. Yes there is. Invisibility. So those that are searching for you just can't see you. So it will save *your* life. And as you learn these things *pass them on*. If you have to say, "I'll teach you for $5,000" I don't care. If someone wants to learn and is willing to pay you $5,000, fine. These lessons *have got to be learned and taught* because not a lot of people will be left in the near future and the knowledge that I'm giving out is for the future people not just us. It is for your children and some of the middle-aged people that will make it through the up-coming Earth flip, the roughly ten million people on this planet left. And they'll need to know this knowledge because we Indians will no longer be here to teach it. No more. There will be no more red man, or black man, or yellow, or olive, or white. In time we will merge to be one color, one language. Part of this is to teach Teleportation because cars and trucks and roads won't be here, to teach Telepathy because no phones are going to exist. But if you can learn these things and *teach* them then you are helping our future race, those few left on our planet when we're all gone to our rewards, to survive the next thirty - forty years that they are going to need to *know* due to the Earth flip. This is why I'm here; this is why I'm teaching. Why don't I give it away? Because I found a long time ago when I give this knowledge out, just give it, it's treated like trash. If you want to throw away your money with the trash you'll think twice about it. That's why I'm selling it. And I spent forty-one years learning it and a number of years doing. This is my JOB. This is the way I make a living.

So my friends, I wish the best to us *all*, not just to those of us on our planet alone but to the others as well. We are wonderful people of all planets. We are wonderful people given wonderful things and only the medicine people of other nations, African, Russian, Norwegian, Laplanders, American Indians, what not, know this knowledge and I've pleaded with my own kind to come forth and start teaching it. So far I don't have anyone who wants to do it. Well, I'm ORDERED to do it. And I sure pray that you've spent your money for a good cause because *you are meant to teach what you're learning now.* Things that we medicine people in general only teach one to maybe five, tops - seven in our lifetime.

This is going out to the masses. You are one of those masses and it's got to go out from you to the others. *Learn it, do it, test it, don't believe a word I'm telling you. Try it. Test me, and then teach it after YOU FIND OUT I speak true.*

Ho,

Red Elk

SELF-HEALING

This segment is on self-healing ways. This will include something of the Hawaiian method, the Kahunas, their medicine people. It's called Ku or Kuing. You won't find it in the library. You won't find it in the dictionary. These are medicine ways from various places, various countries. Before I get too far into it, I'm diabetic and yes I can heal myself. I'm not allowed to. I have to go to others to heal me because in the Inner Heyoka' it is against our rules to do anything for ourselves. We are just not 'self' orientated. Anyway, I'm not you and you aren't me. You don't have to live under my rules, the rules of my people.

HOW TO:

One of the easiest ways of self-healing (on the same identical lines as losing weight the Inner Heyoka' way) is a matter of relaxation, a matter of imagination - going stronger into ENVISIONING - having this 'you' leave. For explanation, you lie down at night at your bedtime (but don't be exhausted), make yourself very comfortable and *relax*. Relax your buttocks, your thighs, the back of your neck, your shoulder blades, everything. Just relax, just melt, or feel like you are being melted into the mattress below you. You want to be just as relaxed as you can be and *still be awake*. In this state with your eyes shut you start *imagining*. Just pretend that you are seeing with your inner eye (your eyes are shut you understand), your brain - your thoughts. With your inner eye you start seeing a 'you', like a shadow, coming out of you and sitting up on the side of your bed. Maybe that 'you' has its fanny connected to you, and it's your fanny or your belly, or what not. As you begin seeing this, then IMAGE it. *Make it stronger.* Make it very, very strong. This Being is a true Being. It is an angel. It's called a Nagual. Tell it, or yourself, the needs. "I really hurt here in this part of my body." What the Being does, you do. If it leans over and starts massaging that arm, or whatever, you physically do the same. You follow the Spirit's directions. If it's making a sewing motion, sew, use your two hands and sew. Always keep your eyes shut. Just follow your own imaging because now it's no longer an *imaging* it's a true blown FACT. You won't see it if you open your eyes, but you will blow it. You will make it disappear the split second you open your eyes. So just relax and do what it's doing. It's not going to hurt you; it is there to help you. You've *asked* for help. This is *one* of the ways the Creator does so. If you can comfortably do it, move your hands with its hands. If it seems like it wants to lift your leg up a little bit, do so. If it's not inconvenient for you, if it doesn't cause you to lose your train of thought, then do it. You are *cementing* what you are actually seeing in your inner eye.

I've seen people that are very, very ill, close to death ill, or at least they thought so, with food poisoning and I explained how to do this and they went about and did it. Now, I can do it too. I can do it for you. But why should I do it for you? You can do it for yourself and hopefully you can teach this to others.

You will feel better. That's all there is to it. It might take two, three, or four days before you really start catching on that you *are* feeling better. Continue on as needed, but don't make it a habit, don't do it seven days a week, four weeks a month unless you are really feeling led to. You don't want to turn it into a *rote* situation or a traditional situation, which is rote. So, break it off every once in a while. Take a rest, try it for about five days (*do it*, don't try), then give it three or four days rest - two or three days minimum, until you can slowly work yourself up until you don't need a rest. Suddenly you are going to be shown *inside* where you are hurt, maybe a torn ligament or something like that and you'll be GUIDED on what to do with it; how to 'mind-bring' the parts together and watch them *weld* together perfectly. All you've got to do is USE YOUR MIND. That's it!

This is also the way that we in medicine do a lot of our work with you people. We go inside, see what the problem is and put it together again for you. Well, these are new ages coming before us. We won't be around anymore. So, this knowledge is being passed on to the world, as they will accept it, so that they in turn can slowly turn around (hopefully, quickly) and *teach* this to their children, their neighbors, their best friends, husbands, and wives, because most of us will be dead in the near future. Those who *teach* this, once they learn it and turn around and teach it, maybe out of the 400 people they happen to know real well, maybe only two will live but they will remember it. They will NEED to remember it to make the next one thousand plus years go by good.

KU METHOD FOR SELF-HEALING

Another way of healing is the Ku, the way of the medicine people, the Kahunas of Hawaii. There's a book, *Suburban Shaman*, and it tells quite a bit about the Ku. But others who have read it tell me they don't get out of it what I get out of it. Of course I am a medicine man and I can kind of read behind the lines and between them. As far as I am concerned, it's a book well worth owning. It's well worth looking into. I like the way the author puts it. He calls the Ku a party animal, and in truth it is. We are made up of three different people. The person you see, the person combing your hair, this we call the Tonal. Then there is the Nagual, the in-dweller of godliness, the angel within

6

us, and then our Soul itself. These are *three actual separate Beings* all working together. You *think* you are seeing one when you go to the mirror but you are seeing *three*. I have to explain this to you to get you to understand what I'm about to explain on Kuing. We give off an essence, an aura. The aura is the *Ku*. This is the party animal. It has no choice; it has to go with us no matter where we go. It has to experience *every* experience that we go through no matter what it is. *It has no choice*. It belongs to you.

HOW TO:

What you can do, if you go to a party and by 'party' I mean an event in your life happens, and you've cut your finger, *if* you can remember *exactly* how it happened, you can *go back into time* mentally re-enacting and re-imaging the accident. I've taught this to many; my daughter, my wife, to many others – I've used this quite often and it works every time. This has happened to my daughter twice and an Indian girl working at a store next door to us. Once she cut her finger really deep, a big V right down to the bone. Well, my friends, there is *no time*, it is only on your wrist, only on the wall, only on the desks and the clocks we use. In TRUTH *there is no time at all*. So, if you cut your finger, all you've got to do is go back and *re-image* the accident itself. Only NOW you want to do it differently. You didn't like cutting your finger in the first place and your Ku didn't like it but that was your 'party', it had no choice. So now, you can go back and RE-LIVE the EVENT, only this time CHANGING the event, CHANGING the past, for the future if you please, and have the knife come *close* (but close doesn't count, doesn't catch you) and IMAGE that *very strong* and do that *time after time*. If you had the accident right then and there, at the time that you start Kuing it will only take three, maybe five times

7

of re-play, re-doing the 'party' before suddenly the pain leaves. You don't want the pain to just lessen you want it *gone*. That's when it has taken effect. The bleeding will stop - everything else will go. Now understand, when you go back to re-do your 'party', do so the same identical way *each* time. Don't change the 'party', it confuses the Ku. Make it identical. Make up your mind, how are you going to miss your finger with your knife, and do it the SAME WAY time after time, after time, until suddenly the pain is gone from your hand. You can wrap a Band-Aid around it no matter how bad it is and when the pain is gone and the blood stops running, the next day (24 hours) you'll wake up and you won't even see an incision from the cut, it just isn't there, *it's unbelievable*! It just never happened. *That 'party' didn't happen.* So your finger is perfect.

Now, in the book, *Suburban Shaman*, the gentleman that wrote it explained an incident where a little boy slammed his hand in the car door. The father (or mother) who knew about Kuing made him put his hand back in the door and then swung the door towards his finger but stopped short. They did this three, four or five times and the pain disappeared on the boy. The 'party' had been re-done by the mother (or father). The boy, I believe, was about five and didn't have the concept of what was going on. Understand, not only the pain was gone but the bruising and swelling that was taking place disappeared right then and there.

Personally, one day, barefoot, I stubbed my toe up against the brick that our wood stove was sitting on and did a big number on it. Oh gee it hurt! Stupidly (I'm not the smartest medicine man in the world), I just let it go. Well, it hurt like crazy for days and suddenly I noticed I was getting blood poisoning. It was not only swelling up but I had to pull the skin away from the side of the toenail where I rammed it in and squeeze my toe to get the pus out and suddenly I saw I was getting a red line up my foot. I was getting blood poisoning. I had no money and like

I said we are not allowed to heal ourselves. There are exceptions to that and that's when you can't get to a healer, be it a white doctor or another medicine person. And in this case this was one of those times. I thought, "What will I do?" and, "What a dummy, just Ku it. I've been teaching everybody else. Do it yourself." So I did. That was maybe fifteen days after the accident so I had to Ku it *many* times, *many times*. When you Ku it right off the bat it only takes three, four or five times but when it's an accident that happened a long time ago then you've got to Ku it, and Ku it, and Ku it, and you go on and on. I think I did it better than fifteen times, if I remember correctly, when suddenly the pain in my toe just turned off. It was gone, so I knew I was okay. The next day it didn't even look like I had ever had an accident. No red blood poisoning on my foot, no swelling on my toe, no pus, no nothing; a nice looking toe for an old geezer like myself. I was very pleased. I gave the Creator great thanks for this. Folks, you have that same ability.

If you buy that book, you'll find that Kuing works on others as well, like that little boy and mother (or father) who *didn't* slam the door on his hand. In another example, the author was talking about some waitress who was really nasty. He could see that she had a black cloud over her head. She was just in a foul mood (a real bad hair day) and he knew she needed help and he didn't need to be served by someone like that either. She went into the kitchen and he 'chased' her with his mind and took hold in his mind of that black cloud. He made the cloud start raining and then made the rain disperse into a sprinkle and then brought flowers and birds and trees above her mind. And she came back and the whole world had changed for her, smiling and happy.

We can do this with our own children. We can do this with our own mates. There is no use to live in misery. We can make things happen, friends. It is all MIND work. It's all WORKING THE DREAM. So, best to you on this, you are going to love

9

this. It works like a charm! But again, make sure when you are doing this, whether it is for yourself or others, that it is the *identical way of going back to the better 'party'.* NO VARIATIONS. Wear the same clothes that you saw in the first 'party'. Settle down exactly what you are going to do. And do it that way EXACTLY until the pain leaves. I don't know if this would work on people who have gotten their backs broken, a paraplegic, or what not. It would take a lot of concentration, a lot of Kuing, but frankly it would not surprise me. If they could actually remember how it all took place, they could go back and re-do it and walk out of there. I'm dead serious.

Ho,

Red Elk

AGE REGRESSION

Friends, you just don't realize the power that you have that the Creator has given you. *Our abilities are so great it's unbelievable!* I've watched many people grow old and die, and I'm growing old. Someday I will age regress but nobody respects a medicine person who has this knowledge and the looks of a young man. So I stay in the pathway of aging. I know better. I know I can do other. I've taught two how to do it. I know of three. The third I've never met but know of her and she appears to be the last I heard, like a sixteen-year-old. Everyone thinks her husband is her grandfather and he's in his sixties and so is she in reality.

There's a fairly recent study that I've heard of where they took older people and put them in a house with the furniture and stuff of their youth, when they were ten, twelve, fourteen years old. They kept these people living there while there was a test group with other people living in their modern homes with all the modern conveniences. They found within a very short while (I believe it was under two weeks) that the people that were in the prepared, old-way house started looking springier and they seemed happier and a very short time after that they were actually looking younger. I don't know how long this experiment went on but from the knowledge that I've been given by someone who does know it went on for a few months. The people that were in that special house (people up in their seventies, and one that was about eighty-one), in just a few short weeks, were looking like they were in their fifties and high forties. Meanwhile the other test group, they were getting older and older anyway, the same old, same old. When they took the people from the prepared house and put them back into their own homes, in less than a week, I guess, they started reverting back and became their plain old selves again. If this is true (what I've been told), science has been working on this phenomenon. But science is way behind those of your own great great ancestors who knew these things.

HOW TO:

The way that I've taught this is to simply get photographs of yourself at various times in your age growth. The closer you can get to a baby picture the better you will be. Then don't get one taken of you just this week or so, but something taken maybe a year or two years ago and progress down in jumps of five or ten years, all the way down to the baby picture. You put these on the table at night. Start with the oldest picture of you, now it's the oldest of all the pictures but it's still a picture of you done two or so years ago, so it's two years younger than you are now. Try your best to find pictures of good memories, happy times. Start contemplating, really *remembering* that moment when that picture was taken, who took it, where were you, how you felt and how wonderful it felt, and so on. When you've DREAMED that picture of the memories, flip it over and go to the next picture down. Do the same thing. When you've *dreamed* those memories of that age, when you were maybe five years younger than the first one, when you've dreamed *all the memories* and how you felt, all the beauty of it, flip that one over. And go on down the line doing the same thing, until you get to where you are in the baby picture. Now chances are you won't remember what it was like other than you felt good. You had to feel good! Maybe you were asleep in your picture. This is the way you go to bed, as a *baby* in BABY MEMORY. That's all there is to it and you wake up in the morning. You go on doing this and after a few days you don't put up the first older picture; you don't use it at all. You go to the one where you were five years younger. Start there and go all the way down to the baby picture, to *baby time*, and go to bed and sleep like a little baby.

The Russian gal, in her early sixties when she started, took about three, to three and a half years to look sixteen. She did this nightly without fail from what I understand. Perhaps there was a sickness or something I don't know, but in general she was very persistent about it. Now, the two I taught, frankly, in a matter of weeks, one of them, a man who I think was about forty-three, was already looking like he was about thirty. He went home to his parents, and hadn't seen them in about a year and according to him he just blew their minds. His brother and sisters just couldn't believe it. "This guy hasn't changed a bit, in fact he's looking a little younger than the last time we saw him!"

So my friends, man is not designed to *die in old age*. Man is designed to die at the calling of the Creator through accidents and illness. I received a phone call from a gal that I taught this to who was real interested in this. She asked me, "Red Elk, is it possible if you do this that all the parts will come back that you've lost?" I think she'd had a hysterectomy. I don't know, I don't know. I know that the Creator is a very wonderful Being and it would not surprise me, it would not surprise me. I can't promise you that my friends. All I can know for sure is you are going to look a lot younger.

Now there is a danger to this. You have got kind of a ball, or big steel wheel, rolling in front of you, that is why you age. You begin as a baby, "When I grow up I can get a bicycle" and you start growing up so you can have a bicycle. "When I grow up I can have a car" and you start growing up so you can have a car. You are always *chasing* the people who are older than you, after what you've seen others out in front of you doing. As a baby you are on your back and your brother and sister come toddling by and you thought, "Gee, when I get their age I can do that" and you did. You started your own wheel turning, and then the tricycle and then the bicycle and then the car and then the job. What happens is that you've got it going so fast, so hard in just your pre-teen and teen years that you aren't aware that you can stop this wheel and back it up. So you go on and on and on aging because you saw mom and dad aging, you saw grandma and grandpa aging and you know you are going to die like them when you get old. You've just started your own wheel, right up to the end of your life.

Now, by reversing that wheel you can go all the way back to a little baby, not in size, but wearing diapers, like in Alzheimer's, so you've got to be careful! When you are *approaching the age you want to be you slow that wheel down*! This time you don't go back to being a baby, or that picture. You drop that one. You go back to the one where you were two years old, the one before you were a baby, and then you start to bring yourself up. You find a balance with what you want between old and young. And you'll swing in looks back and forth. You will have to continue doing these exercises on a continuous basis if you're going to stabilize where you are. It's like a car jerking with too much gas and you are going to go off on one side or the other, just too much. So start putting yourself in neutral until you are satisfied. Give yourself about a three-year life span of what you want to be again. Say you want to be thirty. Will you be happy between twenty-nine and thirty-one? You center yourself. It works! I've seen it work. I've taught it to others and what have you got to lose? Do you think I'm crazy? TEST ME. See how crazy I am. But stick with it until it starts to take effect. People will notice it in you, before you will.

Ho,

Red Elk

LOSING WEIGHT

Friends, this program is on losing weight the Inner Heyoka' way. I was taught this by one of my many Inner Heyoka' teachers and tested it. It works. I can honestly say I used a little bit of it on myself and I went from 293 pounds in a little over a year's time, to what I am now, about 179-182 pounds. My wife had gone to the doctor, my wife's a lovely lady but quite heavy, and they warned her that if she didn't lose weight immediately she would become diabetic. She already had high blood pressure. They wanted her back, if I remember, in about six days. She came home quite upset, tears in her eyes. She doesn't pay a lot of attention to what I tell her on how to do things. She has more white than any Indian blood in her but, nevertheless, she's kind of leery of some of her husband's knowledge. But I said, "Honey if you want to lose weight in a hurry I can tell you how to do it and we can do it in an Inner Heyoka' way." The doctor scared her enough so she decided, at least, she would listen. That night when we went to bed I explained to her what to do and she did it! She carried this out for three days, I believe, just a simple little exercise and she went back to the doctor. She hadn't made any changes in her eating habits. She hadn't made any changes in her physical exercising, which she did and does daily, long walks. She lost eight pounds in six days and the doctor was astounded. He asked her if she had fasted. She said, "No." He asked, "Did you exercise more?" She answered, "No." He asked how she did it. "I just did what I always do." At the time she was not admitting to *anyone* that her husband was a medicine man! So he never found out what it was all about. But he was not only amazed he was very pleased.

HOW TO:

The exercise is very, very simple, and it's possible, *probably*, to *gain* weight on this exercise as well. What you need to do is lie down and relax. You don't want to be so tired that you go to sleep but it's best at night right at your bedtime. It can all be done in your head, you don't disturb anyone around you at all. Let your body just kind of slink down into the mattress. Try to get all of the tension out of you buttocks, out of your legs, everywhere, out of your back, even out of the back of your neck. *Just relax* like you are very warm butter out on the hood of the car, just slowly melting away, bubbling out from above down to below. When you are feeling pretty good about being comfortable, then I want you to, with your eyes shut, envision (*envisioning starts with imagination* so we should say), start imagining that your 'Self' is getting out of your body. I'm not talking about any OBE (out of body experience). 'You' are lifting out of your body, at least a shadow of you. It doesn't have to be anything very specific in color and all that, but just coming up out of your body. As you start *imagining* this, then start getting into the IMAGING of this, the stronger part of imagination. This is the area where it makes imagination become real. IMAGING IS A REALITY MAKER. Always with your eyes shut, command your body to help you lose weight (or like I said, possibly, even gain weight, as you desire). Watch your body, you'll see it in your mind's eye. Keep your eyes shut and it will get up, sit up, pull its legs out of your legs, and put its feet down on the floor while sitting there and it will stand up. It might come out of your feet, it might come out of your head or your mid-section. You'll know it's there. You are making your own little shadow person, but it's your size, it's you, or you think it is. In reality it's your Nagual. Now, you've asked this help to lose weight (or possibly, gain weight) and this Being, this shadow person (there's nothing spooky about this shadow person), is you. It's your Nagual. It's actually an angel inside you coming out of you to do the work you've requested. It will start doing things like maybe it's standing next to you as you are lying there. It might take its hands and dip down into your belly so you can't see its hands. They've literally disappeared inside your skin. Whenever this Being does something physically that you can do without discomfort, you do the same. If it puts its hands inside your belly, you take your physical hands, keeping your eyes shut at all times, and place your hands on top of its hands and press down. Your hands won't go in, the shadow person's will, but yours won't. What you are doing is *solidifying the vision* that you are seeing. When it pulls its hands out and throws something (you might not even see what it is), you do the same. You lift your hands and throw it. If it throws it over its back, you throw it over your back. If it throws it to the left, you throw it to the left, to the right, to the right. If it sets it down beside the bed you set it down beside the bed. You *literally* follow your Nagual's movements as much as you possibly and comfortably can. You want to stay relaxed and you want to be seeing. What this Being is doing is taking out that which you don't need.

In the case of those who want to gain weight, reverse the process. Ask it to put in what you need. Or do whatever *it* deems is necessary for you to gain weight. Again, I don't know if this will work but I don't see why not. Again, do exactly what it has done. If it pulls a green convertible out of mid-air then you too make a green convertible and pull it out of the air. If it rams it front end first into your belly you too do the same thing physically. Again, you are solidifying what you are seeing the Spirit doing. You do this until it is all done. The Nagual will know when it is done. It's finished for that night. It quits and you quit and it just comes back into you or disappears. Actually it goes back into you that way. Do this three nights in a row, four nights in a row. If you can do it a little bit longer, fine. But don't make this a rote habit. Make this a 'called on' need. In just a few short days you are going to be seeing a remarkable difference in your weight structure.

I'm not telling you to go on a diet or eat less cake and candy. I'm not. Meachelle, my wife, just ate as normally as she always does. She didn't hold back a morsel of any food that she wanted to eat. It was not a matter of backing off and going on a semi-diet, fast, or what not. No, she made no changes at all except what she did that night and for two or three nights thereafter. And the results, like I said, eight pounds in six days without her lifting a finger, except 'mind work'. We call this *"working the Dream"*. All this stuff in medicine, we refer to as "working the Dream". It will work. I've seen it work too many times. I've seen it not work, no times. Again, on gaining, I've never even considered it. I've always been trying to lose. But I suppose it will work, just do it in this way and break off, give your Nagual, and your own tonal, human brain - mind a rest. Don't do this every night. It becomes rote, it becomes in a sense *tradition* and tradition is nothing but a bunch of bells and whistles. It is not needed and you don't want to be caught in this. All it does is makes it take more and longer time for you to end up with the same results. Give it a rest after four days, give it a two-day rest or a five day rest, I wouldn't go beyond five days if you still need to lose weight. Then go back after the fifth day and do it again. Until in time, and I do speak from personal experience, you are just not all that hungry and you are getting all the food you want, but that is way out there in time. Anyway, friends, you want to break it up, do it as I advised. Give it a try, it isn't going to cost you an arm and a leg to find out how it works. It is a very satisfying way to lose weight. To those who want to try to gain weight let's see how it works. I'd sure like to hear about it myself!

CURING PHANTOM PAIN

Phantom pain is totally curable, almost instantly. Phantom pain is totally curable, almost instantly.

This cure can be found in the bible and can be explained but it will take too long. There's a way we 12 inner Heyoka cure phantom pain on any amputee body except if your head is disconnected from your body.

HOW TO:

Basically if it itches "the cut off part" scratch it as if it was still there. If you got a leg removed and one of the casts seems to be itchy, pretend as if it is still there and scratch in that spot, even though it's air, scratch at that spot.

If your leg for instance has cramps, massage it as if the part is really there. Be it a toe, a hand an arm a leg; treat it as if it is still in existence. If you can't have someone else do it for you.

In my own case, my large left toe was removed. I did exactly what I'm telling here, just hours after the surgery. The doctor and nurses couldn't believe it that I eliminated the problem. It was them taught as an incurable problem.

I explained what to do.

The nurses in turn, contacted nurse friends of theirs on the east coast and one in California who applied the knowledge to their patients and surgeons. My own surgeon had an amputee with half of a lower leg gone. He personally contacted me to help the guy out. The man's caretaker did the massage work when his leg was cramped, it stopped then and there. The man has been cured and is cured of phantom pain, and I have my surgeons personal recommendation to other doctor's that it works on his own stationary.

A year after my toe was gone, the toe nail of that missing toe, needed to be trimmed. It was starting to cut into my flesh. Though it did not exist, I took clippers to all the other toes, little toe towards the missing big one and clipped that "big one" as well. The problem ceased instantly. That was three and a half years ago and never had to be "trimmed" again.

It's as simple as that. Treat the missing part as if it was not missing. Again this is all bible centered, but it takes way too long to explain it. Do it, spread it, teach it and TRY it! What do you have to lose?

We have many military personnel as well as civilian accidents that need to know how to stop this pain. *Try these things. Test me, and then teach them after* YOU FIND OUT *I speak true.*

Best to you, ho.

Red Elk

INVISIBILITY

All right my friends, this segment is going to be on a form of shape shifting and it is shape shifting, flat out. This is going to be on something I enjoy greatly. I get a kick out of it. I have a ball. I use it more often than I should, but just because it's so much fun. It's how to become Invisible (not be seen by man nor beast) and as you get good, not to be heard. If someone runs in to you, they feel like it was a bump. They don't know they bumped you. They can't see you, smell you, sense you, feel you, hear you; you're totally invisible. It takes practice to hold it for a long time. Well you're here to learn, so practice! This is being transcribed from a tape. The gentleman who was taping this with me (Mike, he's the one that does my web page for me) well, between the last taping that we had just finished on another subject and this, he was kind of laughing at how easy these things are (the telling on how to do them), and I have to agree that the instructions on *everything of medicine* is extremely easy. That does not always mean it's going to be easy to *practice* those instructions. It's like flying, you've got to go at it, and go at it, and go at it until suddenly you're staying up there. Easy instructions, real easy instructions, but to get your mind into it, it's not that simple. Some of these things are. This one's really simple and fun.

HOW TO:

Look at your surroundings. Are you in a living room or in a back yard or out in the woods (or where ever)? Look around you. You want to *be* those surroundings. If you're in the woods you say to yourself, "I am the tree, I am the bush, I am the weeds, the grasses, I am the rocks, I am the dirt, I am the air." If you are in the living room say, "I am the couch, I am the chair, I am the windows, I am the curtains, I am the air, I am the *room*." You're saying this to yourself audibly, now, quietly, but audibly. In time you'll be able to do it without the audible, but this is 101 for you. Same thing works without the audible as you practice. Frankly I've gotten good enough where I just say, "I am the air" and get it over with. No one sees air. They see the wind blowing dust around but you don't see the air and yet it's there because it fills your lungs and it keeps you alive. Much like the Creator, you don't see Him, but he's there, just like the air.

Invisibility is saying those words to yourself over and over and over again until it *clicks into your brain* that you *are* the air, you *are* the tree, you *are* the bush, you *are* the curtain, you *are* the window, you *are* the rug, you *are* the ceiling, the walls, *you are all of it*. You and these things *are one*. And when you click into that you get an enlightened feeling. It's strange. I'm not even sure how to express it but you know that it's true. You look down and you can see your arms and your hands, and your feet and your legs, but you know nobody else can - and they can't. What has happened is you've taken them out of your dreams. And they can walk into a room looking all over for you and you're right there. And the only way they are going to see you is when you GET OUT OF THAT FRAME OF MIND. Now when I do it, I usually say to self, in the head, not aloud this time, "They're going to see me at the count of three. "1 – 2 – 3", and BANG, I'm in front of them! It just scares the daylights out of them. I'm considering using this in some of my talks, pre-

'airify' myself, pre-become invisible, walk up to the mic, and wanting to be heard, allow myself *to* be heard, i.e., "I CAN ONLY BE HEARD, I canNOT be seen, I canNOT be sensed, I canNOT be felt, I can ONLY BE HEARD."   Then I can stand in front of the mic and say, "Good morning folks" and blow some minds. They are going to be looking all over for me. "Where is he?" You can fade in and you can fade out as you get better, like a ghost (all of a sudden, slowly, this form starts to appear and then there you are standing there solid as a rock). I have a lot of fun with this and frankly I like shaking people up and just as frankly, there's times needed that perhaps I ought to prove what I am talking about. I don't like to do that but occasionally it has to happen, I reckon. This might be one of the ways that I'll do it. I'd do it in a gentle way if I do. I don't want to cause any heart attacks. I'll probably pre-warn them over the mic as I'm standing in front of the mic, "I'm in a form of Invisibility, something that all can do so don't be shocked. You're going to see me start to appear now. I will not do it in a snap but I will be in front of your face. I'm going to slowly emerge from the air in front of you where I am anyway." I don't want to get people into a heart attack type situation. All these things you've got to be very careful with. You've got to use these things wisely. YOU might be getting a big kick out of it but you can DO HARM. You can cause people to have heart attacks or faint and fall and hit their head or what not. Be aware of this. Be *wise* on all the lessons that you listen to. *Be very very wise* and think of others. Think of the possible results.   Don't use these things like Invisibility to walk into a bedroom and watch somebody in a sex act. If you do an immoral or ungodly act, you've turned into a sorcerer, and you're using the God power, the God given power, for a *wrong way* and *you WILL PAY for it*! *You will pay dearly for it - s*o be careful. Now that's all there is to becoming Invisible. You have to maintain that thought, "I am air" or what-not, to remain that way. When you want OUT of it, PREset your mind (a kind of kuing). This allows you, on your command, to become visible as you WILL. If you want to scare somebody and you know they haven't got a bad heart, then just pop up in front of them, about five feet away, right where they're looking, right through you, up until NOW. But be careful with these things my children. *Please be careful. Try it. Test me, and then teach it when YOU FIND OUT I speak true.*

Ho.

Red Elk

My friend that's taping this, and I, just chatted for a little while and I thought I'd better add a little bit more to this, just for your sake, to help you understand what you're doing. No matter what it is that I'm teaching you, you are *working the dream*. If you've heard other tapes or discs that I speak on you hear me mention this. The fact is friends, there is only one person, You. The rest are all your imagination, dreams, your own dreams, and it doesn't matter *who you are* if there's two of you, one of you, well actually, each of you are *dreaming* the other. It takes a long time to try to understand this. It takes a long time, a lot of deep thought. But, never the less, when you understand you are *working a dream* then it will help you to understand why these things work. *You are creating your own reality*. It's easy to become Invisible because you take them out of your dreams.

At times, with animals for instance, you can put yourself in a mode where you're not *quite human* and not *quite air*, confusing the animal(s) as they've never seen this before. They're in your dream. You can do what you want with them. In my case, for instance, they come up to me and sniff and smell and I'm doing them no harm. I'm just relaxed there (being a figment of their imagination in a sense). Then I slowly take my fingers and just wiggle them . . . and these very vicious animals start to sniff and think, "Gee, what is this?" Then I slowly take the side of their muzzle and, just like a feather touching the sides of their muzzle, from the side of their mouth I go up towards the back of their cheek, i.e., a caressing. Bears, coyotes, dogs, etc., are familiar with this as that's the way 'mamma' used to lick them. I'm doing this with my fingers. Then I get a little harder and a little harder (this is willing yourself to become physically firmer) and they settle down. It "feels good" (Do you understand what I am saying?). When trying this with animals, do it with a domestic dog, or other pet. With wild animals, don't have FEAR. If you DO show fear and/or if you start showing/feeling fear, you are breaking out of the dream that you have made. And it's quite likely you'll get your butt bit! Understand . . . it can be done. It's all practice. What I do is I will stroke them and become more and more physical at the same time. The animal thinks, "Hey, this is something else. This dream ghost human thing – whatever - it is looking more like a human and gee this touch sure feels good!" I've now got them hooked on the feeling, or if I'm feeding them, I've got them hooked on that. In just a matter of about six, eight, maybe even ten minutes, I'm FULLY formed, FULLY in their reality, and FULLY friends with them and, I can now sit right beside them and actually talk one-on-one *with* them. But that's another matter! Understand, I've never tried this with a Great Russian bear whose eyes are red and teeth are snapping. I'm not that brave, I guess! I'd probably go into Invisibility and get the heck out of there, if it occurred. I don't want to be around a bear when they lose their mind. They're hard to break out via Ku when they are angry and in this insane mind-way. Be careful. This is all future work for you.

All this can be done, from *being nothing* to *being total*. Do you understand? Have fun. As you've learned, do NOT do this for ungodly purposes.

Ho,

Red Elk

LEVITATION

The only reason I'm giving these things out, it's not to make money, it's because, one, I'm ordered, number two, these things are going to be needed in the very near future, especially things like Invisibility. For those who are trying to escape the chases, you might be one of the survivors and you've got to disappear. There's no place to go. There's no place to hide. Yes there is. Invisibility. So those that are searching for you just can't see you. So it will save *your* life. And as you learn these things *pass them on*. If you have to say, "I'll teach you for $5,000" I don't care. If someone wants to learn and is willing to pay you $5,000, fine. These lessons *have got to be learned and taught* because not a lot of people will be left in the near future and the knowledge that I'm giving out is for the future people not just us. It is for your children and some of the middle-aged people that will make it through the up-coming Earth flip, the roughly ten million people on this planet left. And they'll need to know this knowledge because we Indians will no longer be here to teach it. No more. There will be no more red man, or black man, or yellow, or olive, or white. In time we will merge to be one color, one language. Part of this is to teach Teleportation because cars and trucks and roads won't be here, to teach Telepathy because no phones are going to exist. But if you can learn these things and *teach* them then you are helping our future race, those few left on our planet when we're all gone to our rewards, to survive the next thirty - forty years that they are going to need to *know* due to the Earth flip. This is why I'm here; this is why I'm teaching. Why don't I give it away? Because I found a long time ago when I give this knowledge out, just give it, it's treated like trash. If you want to throw away your money with the trash you'll think twice about it. That's why I'm selling it. And I spent forty-one years learning it and a number of years doing. This is my JOB. This is the way I make a living.

So my friends, I wish the best to us all, not just to those of us on our planet alone but to the others as well. We are wonderful people of all planets. We are wonderful people given wonderful things and only the medicine people of other nations, African, Russian, Norwegian, Laplanders, American Indians, what not, know this knowledge and I've pleaded with my own kind to come forth and start teaching it. So far I don't have anyone who wants to do it. Well, I'm ORDERED to do it. And I sure pray that you've spent your money for a good cause because *you are meant to teach what you're learning now.* Things that we medicine people in general only teach one to maybe five, tops - seven in our lifetime.

This is going out to the masses. You are one of those masses and it's got to go out from you to the others. *Learn it, do it, test it, don't believe a word I'm telling you. Try it. Test me, and then teach it after* YOU FIND OUT *I speak true.*

Ho.

If you want to have fun and be safe, I warn you the things that you will be taught in various tapes, they are going to classify you as a witch, a devil, everything that they called Christ, they are going to call you. And you can alienate yourself from these people (from many people) if you are *not sensible, not safe and don't use your head.* Otherwise people won't have anything to do with you. They killed Christ; do you think they are going to do any better to you? I'll tell you, these unusual things *scare* people. This is why we in medicine hold much that is sacred, i.e., secret. People see us as magical, I don't know, anything from devil, to angel, to witch, to God knows all. It's just our natural *Us*. *Everybody's* NATURAL abilities. Period. To us, this is not miracles, to us this is breathing, this is putting on clothes. This is what *we* have learned is *Reality*.

Ho.

Red Elk

HOW TO:

In the many letters I've received since the Art Bell show, I've gotten a number of people who have flown as youngsters, and one who still flies. People *can* fly. Medicine people *do* fly. I've had many complaints, "Why don't you show?" Well, it's *not our way*. We learn it and we leave it. If it's needed the Creator tells us to do it. I will be *commanded only by one*, the commander Himself, my Creator. All right, so far I have had one adult who has learned to Levitate for just over one second. Now that doesn't sound like a long time. It is a start. It is so startling when you do it you drop like a rock. You *know* you've stayed there. Anybody who is watching can see you *stay*. I've taught my grandson. He's been up and stayed up twice. The first time for a little over a full second, the second time for a little over two seconds. He and this adult were doing it together when the adult did it the first time. The adult was just skyrocket high, "I did it, I did it!" Mathew, my grandson, just walked away and shrugged his shoulders. "Big deal, I've done it twice and longer than you."

Basically what you do is you get into the mind-thought of a child, a 2½ to 3½ year old child that can make up people that are real to them. Nobody else can see them but they can party all day and all night with these invisible friends. That kind of an attitude is what you need. *Pretend* that you are flying. Don't pretend that you are *going to* because that's all it will end up being; you are *going to* fly. A 'going to' is not a 'doing'. It is just something in the future.

I started at the age of ten. It was the very first lesson I was given to do and test in my 41 years of training in the medicine ways. Frankly, I was not told what to expect. I was just told what to do and I did it. I stayed up, I imagine a good three seconds. It took me three seconds to realize, "I'm 5 ½ feet off the ground!" That was it. I did it, I knew it, and I tested, and it worked and that's my orders. *You test everything.* If it's true, hold it. If not, discard it. It was fairly easy for me at the age I was, 10 years old, to still have that child-like mind. But, nevertheless, I use the same method for almost all the medicine work I do. I use the simple thing of a trampoline to do this with. I did it off an old beater couch; a big old stuffed couch that was half ripped apart. I jumped off a big old padded arm and jumped onto the pads. At first it was foot-to-foot and then foot-to-belly. I was literally getting unafraid of landing on my stomach. I started out just having fun and that's what you should do, start out having fun. Again, I was not told what to expect. You are being told what to expect. Then I started on this, "Wee, I can fly, I can fly" and that was fun, and I went at this for 20 to 30 minutes easily. And suddenly I switched over from, "I can fly" to saying, "I *am* flying, I *am* flying!" After the fourth or fifth jump saying that, then I stayed up 5 ½ feet from the floor, about four feet from the couch. I stayed there; I locked there, and when it finally dawned on me that I was flying, holy mackerel, I went down like a rock! But I'd learned my lesson.

PEOPLE JUST DO WHAT THEY BELIEVE. Period. *There are only positives.* There are no negatives. "I can't" is a positive. "I can" is a positive. You are *positive* you can't, you 'can not'. So you are *positive* and you WILL NOT because you *are* POSITIVE. Change that to 'can' and be *positive 'can'* and whatever you choose to do, CAN be done.

Because of a lesson given and a lesson learned, I've been able to teach this lesson. Out of all the people who have written since Mr. Bell's show some have asked (many have asked), "What are the directions?" I wish they had gotten it, because my fingers are killing me from writing the directions over and over! The directions are very simple. Get into a child-like mind. Forget that's what you are out there 'trying' to do and just *enjoy being a kid again*. I don't care if you're 50, 55 or 60 years old. Enjoy being a child. If you don't have a trampoline, or any old beater couch or mattress to jump up and down on, go outside and do like Mr. Bell said he did. Run up and down, jumping, *trying to fly*, he said. That is where he got screwed up. You don't TRY, you DO it. It's just when you lose the *trying* and get serious about forgetting about everything except running and jumping and *having fun*, and yelling out, "Wee, I can fly, I can fly", until, "Wee, I *am* flying, I *am* flying" that's when you'll do it!

Now, I like to use scripture as my safety net. If Christ can do it, and He did it, then we can too. He said so. Where did he fly? Well, my friends, walking on water is kind of like flying because that water wasn't ice. That's where he flew, just skimming the surface with his feet. Was he the only man in the Bible that flew? No. Peter was in the boat he was walking to and he said, "If that's you Lord, call me out, let me walk to you." And Christ said, "Come on." Peter got out of the boat and walked towards Jesus until, like I at ten years old, all of a sudden it dawned on him what he was doing – the impossible - and he too went down like a rock. Jesus had to pull him up. So, can people fly? Jesus said you can. You'd better believe it. I've done it.

29

I know personally others that do it - my older sister, quite a woman. She'll wrap her dress around her legs if she has a need to fly. At the time I watched her we were at a bobbed wire fence and it was real muddy down by the gate. It was easier for her to walk to the fence, wrap her dress around her legs, shut her eyes and lift; just slowly and comfortably (she's real good at it) lift. Then she put her mind to send her body forward, she went over the fence, then put her mind to slowly drop down, float, and she did, and went on her way.

The first time, as hard as it is, believe it or not, it's the second time that is the hardest because now you know you've done it. Now you are firmly out there, *trying*. And I tell you my friends, you will trip on *trying*. *It is not going to work*. You're going to spend a lot more time getting back into that child-like mind *forgetting* what you're out there for, just PRETENDING that you are having fun, PRETENDING that you are flying, PRETENDING that you WILL fly, PRETENDING that you're staying up and being a kid again. *THEN* you'll do it again and it will be at least one second longer. Then, down you'll come like a rock. The third time is probably as hard as the first time. But once again, using the same method I've told you here, you will go up, you will stay maybe three or more seconds longer. Then, down like a rock. There is an odd thing about the number three. If you can do it *three times*, then you have *broken* what we call the *tonal brain*. The brain that says, "This is reality. I put on my clothes, that's reality. I drive the car, that's reality." You have changed your brain to the Reality of the spiritual side of you. What *you* think is reality, you open the door and walk out. *We* know better in medicine. *This is not Reality. Dreams and being able to fly* – that's TRUE *Reality*. The rest of it well that's another story and something very few white people understand at all let alone know. So to *us*, flying is not a miracle. Flying is simply a Reality beyond the norm - or reality to you because you don't know how to do it. You are full of your 'can't(s)'. Your mom and dad, your peers, say, "Oh you can't fly" and you've accepted that positive saying that they say. 'Can't' is a *positive* word. When you can get rid of those 'can't(s)', that positive "I can't", and get into the positive "I can" my friend, you WILL. Period. You will fly. Now it might take practice but as long as you keep in the POSITIVE, it WILL happen no matter *what it is you are after*!

Please be careful with this knowledge because you can do evil as well as good. It will happen, if you are positive about it. I'm ordered to teach and I guess it is really up to the Creator to let you go bad versus good. I pray for your sake and for the world's sake that you use this only for Godliness, and only for love, and only for *right reasons*. But that's your path. Now, say you've done it three times. You've really worked at it. Your mind is now set on the great (more than probability, you've done it, more than possibility, you've done it) thought, 'you can fly'. You have re-geared your mind from 'can't' to 'can'. Therefore it's easier to do it the fourth, fifth, sixth time, until literally, if you keep at it, keep practicing, you can walk through your living room without running and jumping and *rise* like my sister does!

Beyond 101 Levitation

Now, there is more to this. We are going past 101. We are going into height, speed, and direction. All it is, is a matter of *thinking* the direction you want to go. *Thinking*, how fast you want to be there, or how fast you want to go as you are in your raised position. Do you want to sit down? As I told Mr. Bell, you can sit down in an imaginary car seat, put your arm through an imaginary window, (like you are resting your left arm out the window) put your right hand on an imaginary steering wheel, and go 70 miles an hour past the people on the freeway.

31

There's nothing there but you. Now understand, is that a wise thing? *No* it is not. You can cause accidents, you can cause heart attacks. BE SMART about what you are doing. *This is why we don't show off!* Come on, use your head. Think of others, not just yourself. Again, *think* the direction you want to go. Do you want to do it like Superman lying down? *Think* yourself in that position. Think it slowly, comfortably. Don't think "I'm going to lie down" and bang, you're lying down. That will shake you up so much you will drop again. No, be casual about it, piece of cake. This is just like picking up a Sunday cookie. Take it easy. Then, when you are in the position you want just say, "Stop" and pivot to the left slowly, comfortably, or to the right, or behind you, then turn around. Pivot slowly and comfortably, especially as you are learning this so you don't frighten yourself and drop.   Once you're in the direction you want and you want height, you can say, "I want to be higher." But remember, if you're doing this in a house you do have electric light bulbs up there, you do have things you can bump your head on. You can slam your head into the ceiling because you haven't given yourself an order on how high to be. So be *very conscious* of what you are doing, *very deliberate*, *very calm*, and *very precise* on what you're after and it will *be*. Period. Then you can go from there. There are other ways to learn flight. I've given you the easiest basic kindergarten 101 on how to Levitate.

If someone is listening and is *really* advanced, stand there, raise your arms like you are praising the Creator, shut your eyes, and thank the Creator, literally thank Him for what He is allowing you to do now. Then simply spread your arms out to your sides, like a cross, and calmly think that you are floating and start leaning back, falling, straight legged, straight backed. If you are that advanced your body will catch, as if on a cushion of air, before it hits the floor, and then you can slide up to the position you want, feet first, and then you can go about doing the other things.

There are people who do fly unintentionally and unexpectedly. We call this 'panic flight' or 'need flight'. The Creator knows your needs and so do you. You have to get to that baby rolling down the stairs! You jump past it, suddenly you twist in the air, you land on the floor, catch the baby, you've landed on your knees and didn't feel a thing. You *flew* past the baby. You *floated* to your knees at a very fast speed and you landed like any bird that takes to a branch and comes down. So this is 'fright' or 'need flight' and there's not anything you can do about it. You can't train yourself to do that uncontrollable flight. It's like a lot of people uncontrollably going to OBEs (out of body experiences) and they have no choice. It just happens and this is one of the ways it happens.

So, my friends, that is it, plain and simple. Test me. See if I'm true. I know I am. Others know I am. Many will not do this because they *don't get into the right frame of being, the 'true child' pretending way of it*. If you keep that hidden knowledge, "I'm going to *try* to fly" you are not going to get any higher than you can jump, period, and you will fall right back down. THIS DOES WORK. We don't need cars, planes, trains, busses, boats, or spacecraft. Good luck, keep in touch, let me know when you are up. Don't hit any light bulbs. You can not only get glass in your hair you can get electrocuted. *Don't be stupid*.

Try it. Test me and then teach it after YOU FIND OUT I speak true.

Ho.

Red Elk

TELEPORTATION

This lesson is on teleportation. Again, I use the Bible. Has it been done there? Yes. One of the apostles was strolling through the desert, I guess, and some eunuch was reading the Old Testament aloud as he was riding in his chariot and this apostle heard him and ran up to him and said, "Do you know what you are reading?" And the eunuch said, "How would I know without somebody teaching me?" The apostle jumped in the chariot and taught him. During the teaching they were coming to some water and the eunuch asked, "What's to keep me from being baptized?" The apostle said, "Nothing." So they stopped the horse and walked over and the apostle baptized the eunuch. Scripture says that *immediately* afterwards the apostle *appeared* in a distant city –

Teleported. If I remember correctly, the eunuch went on his way praising the Creator. Yes, it was in the scriptures. So, yes we can do it. Now, the directions for Teleportation (you are going to laugh) are only a matter of a few short words. *Knowing* the directions and *doing* the directions are two different things.

HOW TO:

If you want to go somewhere, *think* where you want to go with your eyes shut. Go there, open your eyes and be there. This is the direction on how to teleport. Now practice that one. We do this very, very little. We do it only if ordered once we've learned. A few foolish people do it more than that. There's a reason for being careful. It is extremely dangerous. Go into your living room, get rid of the coffee table, push everything up against the wall so you've got a big landing area so that when you appear you have a safe place, you're not banging onto a coffee table or something. Make it safe. *Eyeball* that area. *Know* that place, *know* that section of rug, or what not, *know* where you are going to land. *Know it!* Know it as well as you know your own hand. *Ingrain it in your head*. Get it so that you can shut your eyes and know where the window is, where the picture is on the wall, where you are going to end up standing when you get there. You KNOW it. It's not a matter of, yes this is where I'm going to be, it's a matter of *knowing* that is where you are going to be. Therefore you're safe. Make sure no cats or dogs are going to wander through. You can actually (this has happened) end up with a foot in the coffee table-not on it, in it-or in a dog, *in it*. Do you understand what I mean? Wherever you appear, you are coming back *solid*. If there is something solid there in your way, it is going to be part of you. I tell you, this is dangerous. I mean it.

When it is needed to be done, we've learned what we call 'spirit travel'. This is not an OBE (out of body experience). It is a form of going in spirit, being fully aware of where we are and doing whatever we need to do. We 'split'. We send ourselves to where we want to go, in spirit. We are really there, we are two people. The physical *here* and the spirit *there* - wherever 'there' is. We check out the area thoroughly. I would not go long distances if I were you. It's stupid. You don't know how to do this 'splitting'. You might think you want to be at this lovely park setting where you visited five years ago. You have it all imaged in your head. Well you go there all right, and that park is gone. Instead there is an eighteen-wheeler bearing down on you in the middle of a freeway. It is dangerous. How much stronger can I put it than that? This is nothing to play with. It is something to learn and use ONLY if necessary.

So you've got it all squared away. You definitely have the whole area where you are planning to go back to strongly in mind. Then go into your bedroom, lie down or sit in a chair, relax, just relax. And I do mean *relax*. Make your body as if it is melting butter - not sizzling hot but melting, spreading out beneath you in relaxation. Shut your eyes as you do this, feel good about yourself. Be relaxed-relaxed-relaxed. *"This is where I want to go. This is where I want to be. This is where I will be. This is where I am right now."* Open your eyes and you should be there. It's that simple. I'll tell no more. In taping this I was asked, "Then is it better to go in spirit than physically?" Definitely, yes. I can go in spirit and never get in trouble. I can get run over by an eighteen-wheeler. I am not even seen by that driver, I am a ghost. I'm just a wisp of thought. *Please be careful. Try it. Test me, and then teach it when YOU FIND OUT I speak true.*

Ho.

Red Elk

TELEPATHY

This segment will be about "on demand" Telepathy. We all have experienced it, at least anyone beyond the age of seven, eight or ten. The kind of Telepathy where you might be in a car and think, "Boy, I'd like to get a Dairy Queen or what not, and the other person says, "Yea, I was just thinking about that!" It is mind transference of one thought to another. We all, in some way shape or form have experienced it to a minor degree. So you know telepathy *is* in existence. There should be no problem with anybody otherwise. Now, *knowing* that you do it on rare occasions is one thing. DOING it *"on demand"* is quite another. It's a fun thing to do. You're going to love this one!

HOW TO:

You get a partner, choose one person (you can choose up to two others besides yourself but this causes too much excitement). Stick with one. Go to an area that is really clear, like a wall that has nothing on it. Or, put a bed sheet on it, dead white, so that you are staring at nothing but this total nothingness—whiteness (or whatever color that you choose). Don't get anything busy like flower prints. Believe it or not, it wavers your mind-thought. Two of you stand side by side, don't touch each other it's not necessary. One's going to send and one's going to receive. Both of you close your eyes facing this wide-open place. Make certain there are no distractions. No phones. No kids running in and out. A quiet place. Side by side, both of you shut your eyes facing this wall of nothingness. One is going to send and the other is going to receive. The sender is going to visualize a simple scene or object like a red ball. Keep it very simple, don't make anything complicated. You are just starting out on this. Visualize a ball, any color you want. Make it very *vivid*. First you start with imagination. Then image it until you can almost *taste* that ball, *feel* that ball, *smell* that ball *turning* in your hands. All five senses go to work at this, you see. *Make it that* REAL. Then project that *real thought*, "ball", onto the wall. Just *think* it like it is *at* the wall and then say, "I'm ready." The person next to you is clearing their mind, getting ready to receive. Your, "I'm ready", means the object to be received is *THERE*. They, in turn, audibly tell you what they see. They might see an object, a round object. They might not even see color. But they got the round part right. Or they might see the color red without the ball. That's still a good point. They are on the right track. You can ask them if there is anything in particular about the red. *Keep your ball in mind*. They close their eyes and say, "Well it's round. I think it's a red ball." Now you can trade places, not physically, but now he or she will be the sender and you the receiver and you repeat the process. It's just about 99.99 percent sure that the FIRST thing the receiver gets in their mind is right on the money. *Don't hesitate saying what you see the* FIRST TIME. Otherwise, you'll start making little imaginary tricks in your own brain. If all you see is color, give it. If all you see is round, give it. Whatever.

Now me, when I do this I make it a three-peaked mountain with snow caps and the people always get it. They'll say, "It's a mountain or hill" and I'll say, "Good, good! Can you tell the difference?" I'll put the image back in my mind. They'll then say, "It looks like a mountain." They will see a mountain but not three peaks. Then I'll say, "Is there anything about the mountain?" while focusing really hard on the three peaks. "Three peaks, three peaks" seeing it and thinking it. Then they will see the three peaks. Then I will ask, "Is there anything about the three peaks?" And they see the snow covered peaks.

I say, "Well, you got it right on the money!" Trade places but don't give each other the same thing. Make it very, very easy. When I taught this one time, the student tried to send to me and I looked at him and I said, "I told you to make it easy." He had a guy pedaling like crazy on a bicycle. I said, "Now this next one you make it easy. Make it a stationary, simple object like a triangle, a ball, or a doghouse, and not a fancy one." *You make it easy.*

Now, you can do this with each other two times in a row and you'll be right two times in a row. The third time, you *may* be right, but the chances are you won't be. You will be too far off. Close but not close enough. So stop doing it. You are done for the day (for that 24 hour period). Don't get together again to do this at all for five days, six or seven is fine, but don't make it too long afterwards. Then get back and do the same thing again. Once again, the first two times for each of you will work like a charm but the third time may not. Stop again for five days. Get back together again, and try it again. This time, one, two and three will be true but the fourth one might cause some problems. Stop. You can get up to four times accurately and then five will cause a problem. Take a break, only this time go only three, maybe four days and then try it again. What you are doing is *'can-ing' your 'can't(s)'*. You are re-aligning your brain. You are making your brain realize it is not *stuck* in its 'can't' mode. You are *re-training* yourself. So, five times, fine, six times, fine. When it starts to waver, get away from it. Over a period of about a month and a half to two months, you'll be able to play this back and forth like badminton.

Now, when you have that downright you can find a place that your are both familiar with, that you have both visited, that you are both comfortable with, like the backyard of someone's house or a park. Go home separate and arrange a meeting, by mind, for a certain time, on a certain day each week say, Wednesday night at seven o'clock. You will want your partner to pick up the mental phone when you are ready. What you do, once you are ready, is send your face, or a thought like, "Hey Jill are you ready?" You jar them into memory. They should do it too. Both of you simply, where ever you are at, visualize the place where you have agreed to meet. SEE *you going into that place. Visualize* YOU there. See an image of you *going there*. Then SEE an image of your talking partner coming in. And then sit down and talk and have a normal conversation. Then break up, come home in spirit, open your eyes and call each other that night or the next to see what part you got right and what part you got wrong. You are re-training your mind from a distance. You will be amazed at how much accuracy was involved! Keep practicing this. Now, you don't need to wait three or four days for this. You can do it the next night and the next night after that and so on. Then, say your calling partner happens to call you up on the phone and says, "I've got to fly to Africa. I'll be there a week." You set up a time (their time in Africa and your time in the States) and agree on that time and go for it. You don't have to call back and forth. By then you are probably good enough to know what you are talking about. Now you might not even need that 'space' anymore. Now when all of a sudden you get an image of your call partner, that partner's calling you or in need of help and you pray for them. Go and see what they need. *Mentally go.* Bill has a need. Mary has a need. This is 'splitting'. Where are they? The Creator knows, ask Him. "Send me to them so I can see what their need is" (if it happens to be that kind of urgency). He'll let you *see* them. *Accept* what you see. Or if there isn't that urgency, you know it's a phone call instead. Call them right back and have yourselves a conversation! They can be on *Mars* and you can have this conversation!

Now once you've learned this and your partner has learned this, find others. Break up into another partner, both of you, so that now four of you know this. Banter back and forth between the four of you. Let all four of you go to others, and then you've got eight, and it skyrockets! The next thing you know AT&T, Mr. Internet nosey busy body, is wondering what has happened. Did you die? Well they haven't learned to read your mind yet. Not mechanically 'on demand'. They can do it but you have to be in the room with the machine aimed at you. And they don't have enough mind readers in the 'black government', or any other government, to cover everyone in the United States. If you're really good, make a code so if and when they do learn how to read your mind they can't figure out your code. You can block it. You can put up a mental door with a code in it. You know the code and they can't get in to get it. It's really cool, people. We've got too many men in black, I don't know - too many people minding my business and not their own. We can overcome these twits. All right, that's it. Good luck. You're going to have fun with this one!

Try it. Test me and then teach it when YOU FIND OUT I speak true.

Ho,

Red Elk

Red Elk

ABOUT THE AUTHOR

Red Elk is a Metis Medicine Man, and member of the Inner Heyokha. Red Elk is a Wakhan, a Spiritual Adviser (similar to a priest/preacher) which is a called position. Red Elk states, "YOU DON'T NEED ME. Never really have. You who want to know the Inner Heyokha Way can find that way in "The Good Book" (WITH Concordance), and connecting to The Great Creator with FULL TENACITY.

This will not make you an Inner Heyokha...but VERY CLOSE. It CAN be done...and IS!

"FOLLOW ME" (Big Brother) and you will grow to the Inner Peace we twelve have.

We call this: "PURITY". Aho? Alright, unless ordered otherwise, I've done all I can do. I WISH YOU ALL WELL. We ARE: "ALL one RELATION".

Ho.

Red Elk

Red Elk

A MESSAGE FROM ADAM

Medicine people live and practice a way of life very different from others. Each doing medicine things differently and have their own specialties. In general there is a universal way to interact with a medicine man. Tobacco is given as an acknowledgement of who you're working with (Red Elk prefers Pall Mall No Filter). Also, a medicine man smokes and or prays with the tobacco. This is done to make a decision on whether to take on your problem or answer your question. And yes, sometimes the answer is "no". A donation is given equal to the problem or question. Some medicine people have a standard fee i.e. 100 dollars. Red Elk is an Inner Heyokha medicine man and does not have a standard fee. A person is required to pray and connect with Dad (GOD) to determine the amount to be donated. This is practiced so everyone in the tribe has the same access to spiritual and medical care (rich or poor). This is observed every time a person interacts with medicine people asking for a healing or question.

A medicine man/woman will use the years of learning and experience along with time and energy to help solve the problem. The donation is an exchange in energy. His/her time and energy to help solve your problem in exchange for your donation. In this case, there is no difference between a buffalo hide and dollars, both provide a way to exchange energy. After all, we are all family.

Adam

PS: This might be a good time for Red Elk to share the story of the original 13 Inner Heyokha and why there is only 12 now.

Made in the USA
Lexington, KY
27 March 2016